CONCERT REPERTOIRE FOR
TRUMPET
(B♭ TRUMPET/CORNET)
with piano

edited, selected and arranged by
ausgewählt, herausgegeben und bearbeitet von
choisi, édité et arrangé par

Deborah Calland

© 2007 by Faber Music Ltd
First published in 2007 by Faber Music Ltd
3 Queen Square London WC1N 3AU
Cover illustration by Drew Hillier
Music processed by Jackie Leigh
Printed in England by Caligraving Ltd
ISBN10: 0-571-52543-1
EAN13: 978-0-571-52543-0

To buy Faber Music publications or to find out about the full range of titles available
please contact your local music retailer or Faber Music sales enquiries:

Faber Music Limited, Burnt Mill, Elizabeth Way, Harlow, CM20 2HX England
Tel: +44 (0)1279 82 89 82   Fax: +44 (0)1279 82 89 83
sales@fabermusic.com   fabermusic.com

FABER *ff* MUSIC

CONTENTS

Loudly let the trumpet bray

from *Iolanthe*

Arthur Sullivan (1842–1900)
arr. Calland

5

March

from the overture to *Atalanta*

George Frideric Handel (1685–175
arr. Calla

Bamboogled

Deborah Calland (born 196.

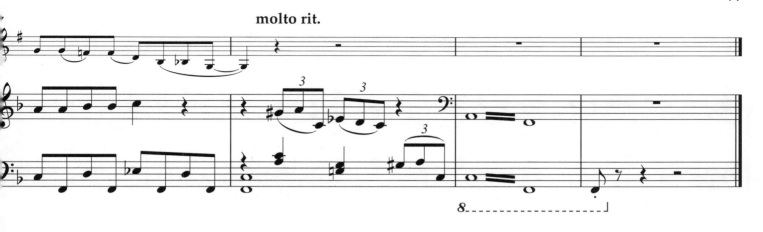

molto rit.

Solace: A Mexican Serenade

Scott Joplin (1868–1917)
arr. Calland

Tempo di tango ♩ = 60

Blues from *An American in Paris*

George Gershwin (1898–19

arr. Call

Andante ma con ritmo deciso ♩ = 69

Grave and Allegro
from Sonata in D for trumpet

Arcangelo Corelli (1653–171
arr. Calla

Donna Anna's Revenge

('Or sai chi l'onore') from *Don Giovanni*

Wolfgang Amadeus Mozart (1756–1791)
arr. Calland

Andante con moto ♩ = 112

CONCERT REPERTOIRE FOR
TRUMPET
(B♭ TRUMPET/CORNET)

Trumpet part

CONTENTS

FABER ff MUSIC

Loudly let the trumpet bray

from *Iolanthe*

Arthur Sullivan (1842–1900)
arr. Calland

March
from the overture to *Atalanta*

George Frideric Handel (1685–1759)
arr. Calland

Bamboogled

Deborah Calland (born 1965)

Solace: A Mexican Serenade

Scott Joplin (1868–1917)
arr. Calland

Blues from *An American in Paris*

George Gershwin (1898–1937)
arr. Callan

Grave and Allegro

from Sonata in D for trumpet

Arcangelo Corelli (1653–1713)
arr. Callan

Donna Anna's Revenge

('Or sai chi l'onore') from *Don Giovanni*

Wolfgang Amadeus Mozart (1756–179
arr. Callar

Theme from *Rhapsody in Blue*

George Gershwin (1898–1937)
arr. Calland

Nimrod

from *Enigma Variations*

Edward Elgar (1857–1934
arr. Callan

to the victims of the Port Arthur massacre, Tasmania, 28 April, 1996

In Memoriam

Peter Sculthorpe (born 192?
arr. Callan

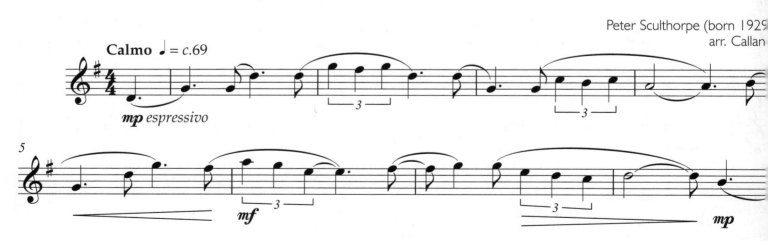

The Spider and the Fly

from *Johnson over Jordan* Suite

Benjamin Britten (1913–1976)
arr. Callan

Danse Bacchanale

from *Samson and Delilah*

Camille Saint-Saëns (1835–1921)
arr. Callan

Allegro
from Concerto in D for trumpet

Georg Philipp Telemann (1681–1767)
arr. Calland

CODA

Theme from *Rhapsody in Blue*

George Gershwin (1898–193
arr. Calla

23

Nimrod

from *Enigma Variations*

Edward Elgar (1857–193
arr. Calla

to the victims of the Port Arthur massacre, Tasmania, 28 April, 1996

In Memoriam

Peter Sculthorpe (born 19...
arr. Calla...

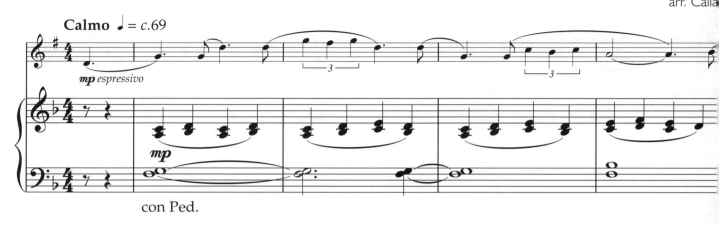

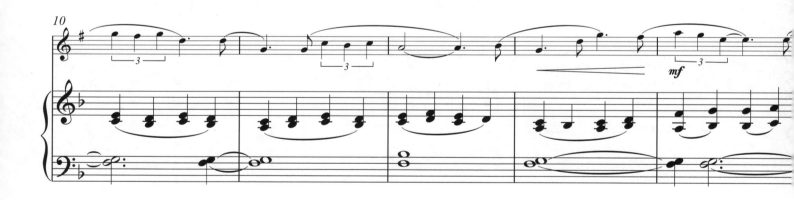

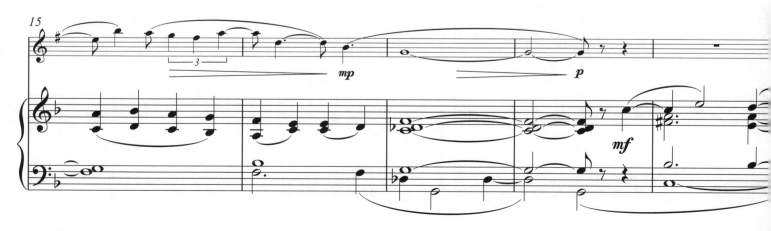

36
poco f
mf
mf
40
mp
mp
44
mf
mf
48
meno mosso
mp
mp
p
dim. a niente
L.H.
Ped.

The Spider and the Fly

from *Johnson over Jordan* Suite

Benjamin Britten (1913–1976)
arr. Calland

Allegro vivo [♩ = 88]

Danse Bacchanale

from *Samson and Delilah*

Camille Saint-Saëns (1835–192⌐
arr. Calla⌐

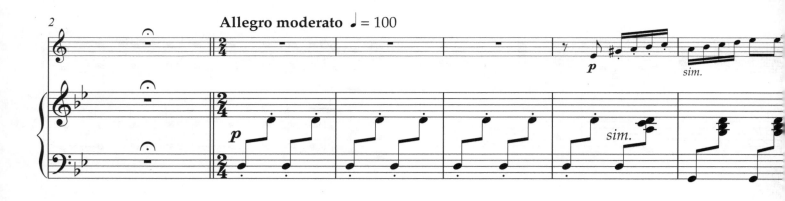

Allegro
from Concerto in D for trumpet

Georg Philipp Telemann (1681–176
arr. Calla